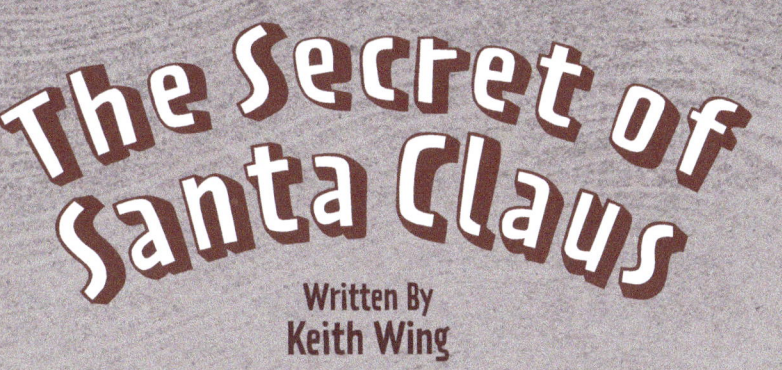

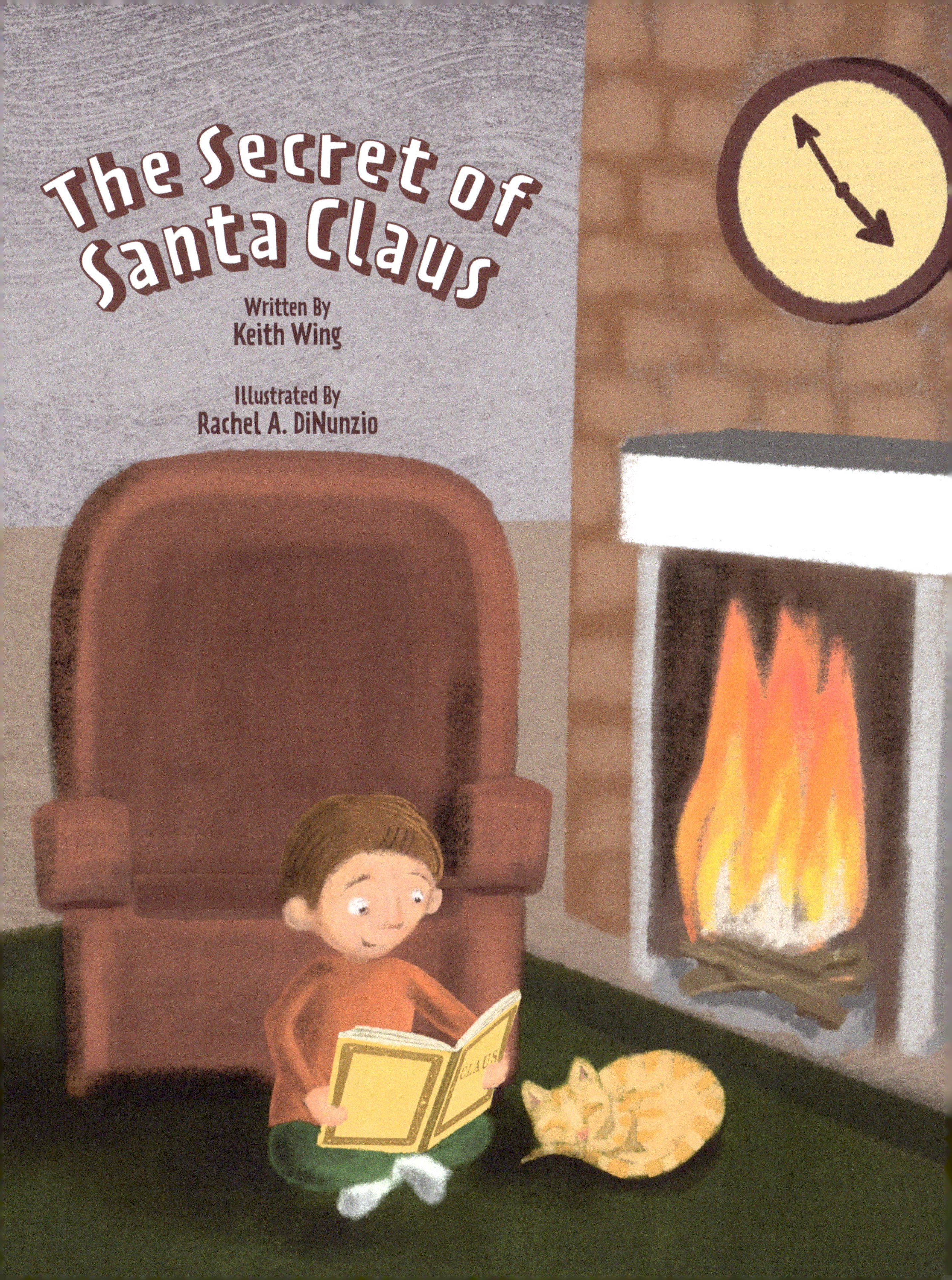
The Secret of Santa Claus
Written By
Keith Wing
Illustrated By
Rachel A. DiNunzio
CLAUS

Dedicated to Ethan, Jillian, and Andrew

No part of this publication may be reproduced in whole or in part, or stored in a retrieval system, or transmitted in any form by any means, electronic, mechanical, photocopying, recording, or otherwise, without written permission of the Author.
For information regarding permission, write to thesecretofsantaclaus@gmail.com.

Follow on Instagram @TheSecretofSantaClaus

ISBN: 978-1-941475-40-9
Library of Congress Control Number: 2021903061

A Library of Congress Registered Document

Text and illustration copyright © 2021 by Keith Wing
Illustrations created by Rachel A. DiNunzio,
RachelDiNunzio.com

All Rights Reserved. Published by Keith Wing

Published in Buffalo, NY
Printed in the USA

First Edition

After a long day,
Michael stumbled in through
the front door of Grandpa's house.

Grandpa always cared for Michael and his little sister on Friday afternoons while his parents were still at work.

School that day had been normal, until something shocking happened that made Michael question everything.

Instead of heading straight to the snack cupboard, Michael sat slumped at the dining room table.

"Is everything all right?" Grandpa asked.

"Not really," sighed Michael.

Michael stared at the Christmas drawings he and
his little sister had made the week before.
A decorated green Christmas tree.
A bright red sleigh with golden bells.
His baby sister's crayon hurricane that only
a toddler could create.

"Grandpa, today at lunch, Bridget Mayfeld told me that there is no such thing as Santa."

"Grandpa, is Santa Claus real?"

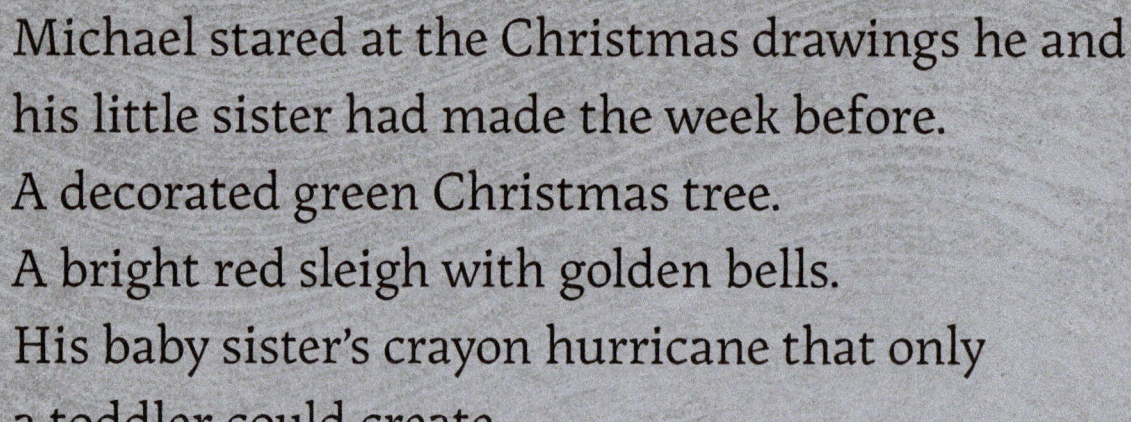

Grandpa looked at Michael with thoughtful eyes. "Michael, I guess now is as good a time as any to tell you the truth."

Michael held his breath, preparing for the grandest of let downs. It was one thing for Bridget Mayfeld to break his heart, but it would be another for Grandpa to do it.

"You see, Michael, at some point everyone starts to wonder about Santa Claus. Could something so magnificent be real? Well, let me share a special secret with you."

Grandpa plodded over to his bookshelf. "Now, where is it?"

Grandpa gently slid a book off the shelf and handed it to Michael.

It was an old, leather-bound text. One word was written on the cover in faded gold: *Claus*.

"This book was given to me many years ago. It describes, in detail, the great history of the blessed men who have been given the honor of being Santa Claus."

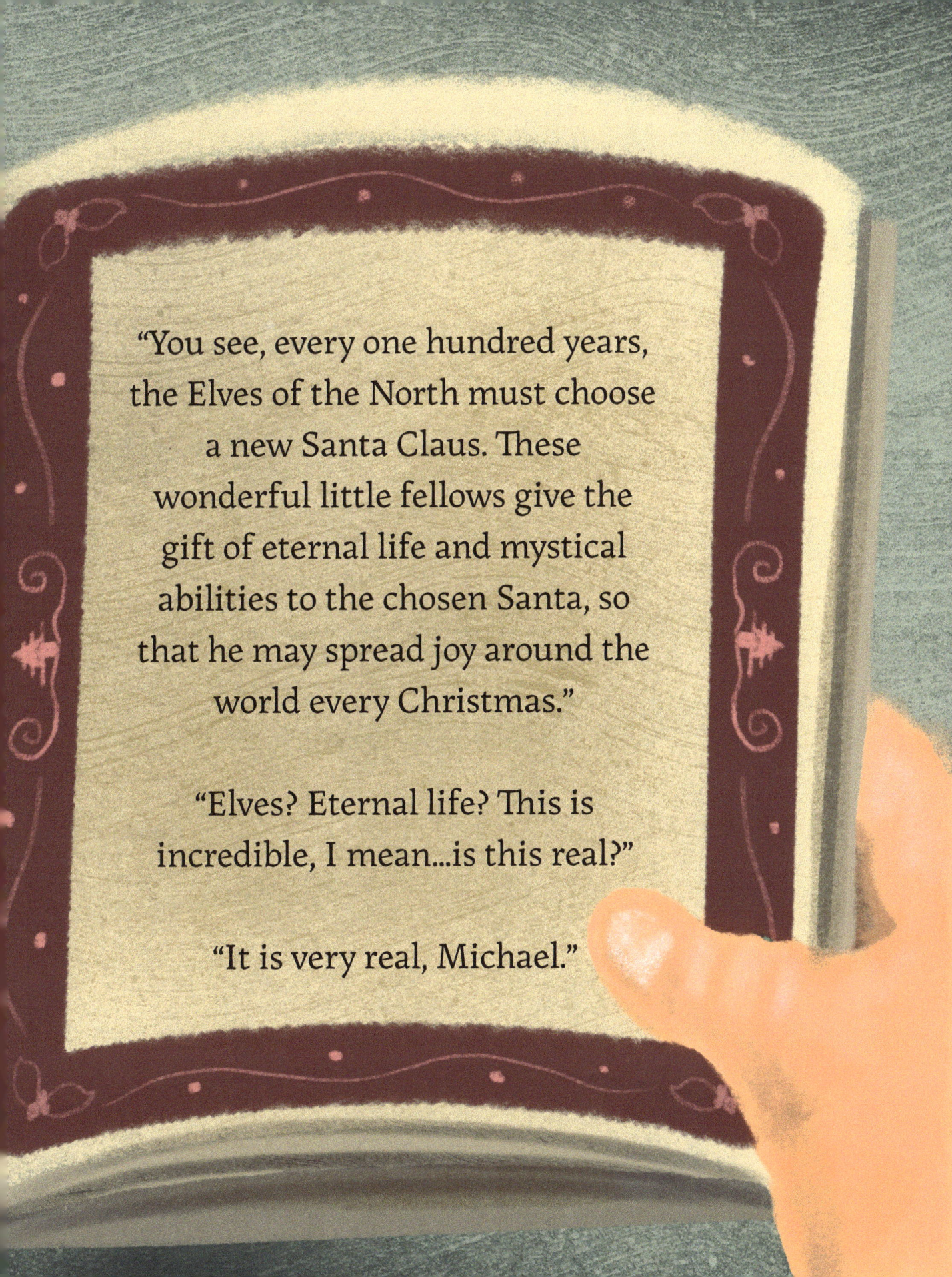

"You see, every one hundred years, the Elves of the North must choose a new Santa Claus. These wonderful little fellows give the gift of eternal life and mystical abilities to the chosen Santa, so that he may spread joy around the world every Christmas."

"Elves? Eternal life? This is incredible, I mean…is this real?"

"It is very real, Michael."

The book had page after page of great, kind men from around the globe who were chosen to be Santa. Michael carefully inspected the pages in amazement.

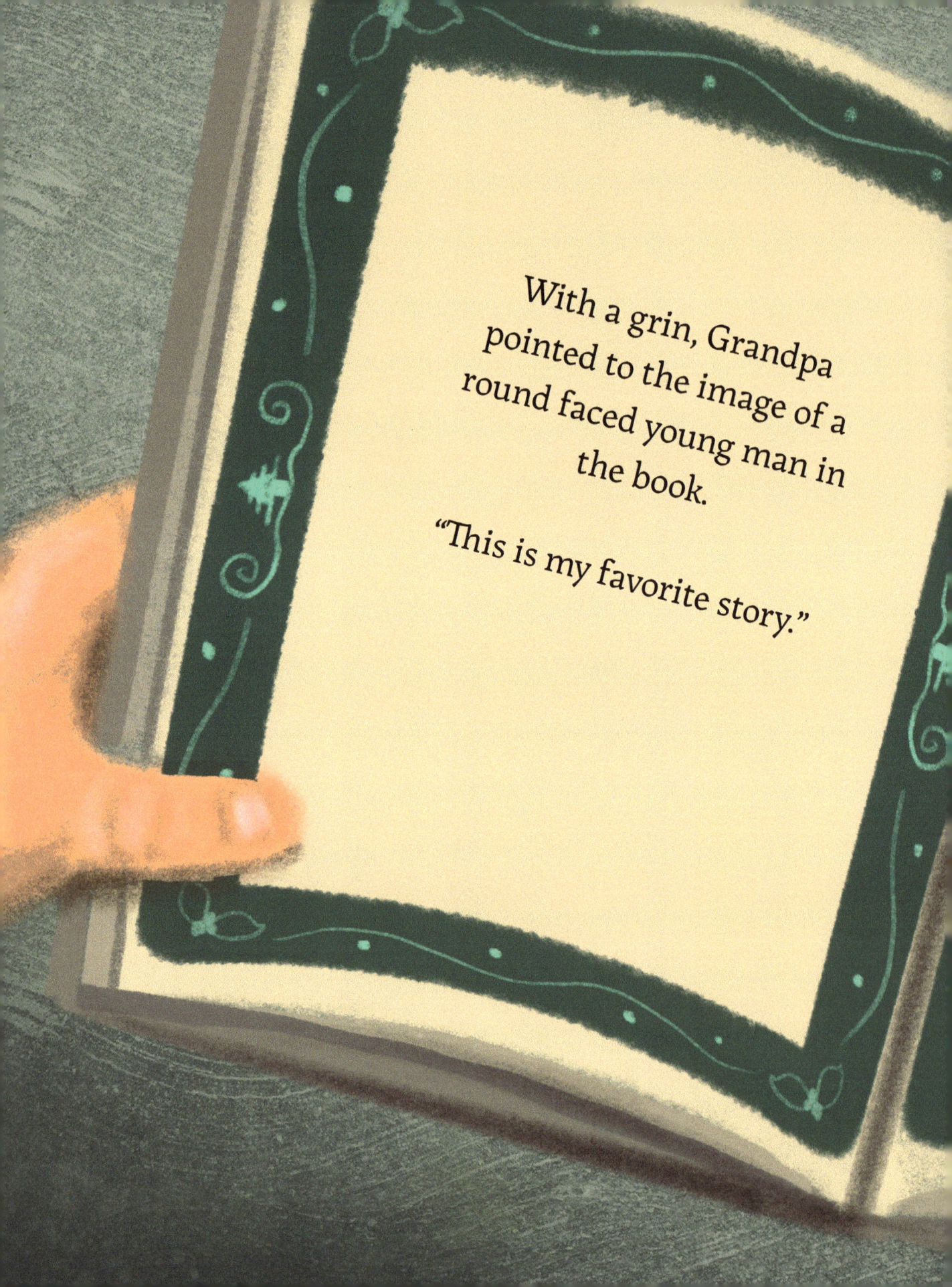

With a grin, Grandpa pointed to the image of a round faced young man in the book.

"This is my favorite story."

"That fella there was Henry Hudson. Your teachers will tell you he was a great explorer. Maybe he was, or maybe he wasn't. I'm not really sure.

I do know that he was not only fortunate to have been a Santa, but he was lucky to have even survived. You see, he was found by the Elves on a sheet of floating ice near the Arctic in 1611. The Elves rescued this soul and taught him about love, giving, and the magic of Christmas. They say he was a fine Santa Claus."

Michael looked at the image closely.
"I don't know why, but he looks familiar."

"Is that so?" asked Grandpa with a look of amusement.

"Here's the deal, kiddo...in your lifetime you will find people who don't believe in the magic or wonder of Santa Claus. But I know the truth. And now, so do you."

Michael felt great joy in his heart, and he couldn't help but smile.

Michael heard his father's car pulling into Grandpa's driveway and carefully slid the old book back onto the shelf.

Still in awe of what he had just learned, Michael gave Grandpa the greatest of hugs.

As Michael and his sister got ready to go home, he had one more question for his grandfather.

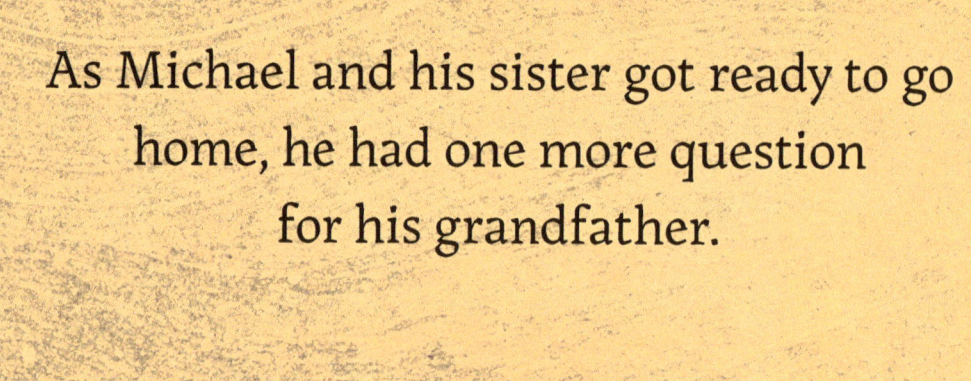

"Grandpa, have you ever met Santa Claus?"

Grandpa winked. "Of course I have, but that was a long, long time ago."

The End

CPSIA information can be obtained
at www.ICGtesting.com
Printed in the USA
BVHW021400110122
625983BV00006B/861